pocket
cornwall

Walking on the Lizard

David Chapman

Alison Hodge

First published in 2014 by
Alison Hodge, 2 Clarence Place, Penzance,
Cornwall TR18 2QA, UK
info@alison-hodge.co.uk
www.alisonhodgepublishers.co.uk

ISBN-13 978-0-906720-93-6
British Library Cataloguing-in-Publication Data
A catalogue record for this book is available from
the British Library.

Designed and originated by
BDP – Book Development and Production,
Penzance, Cornwall

Printed in China

Title page: Church Cove, Lizard peninsula

Abbreviations

NCI	National Coastwatch Institution
NNR	National Nature Reserve
NT	National Trust
SSSI	Site of Special Scientific Interest

Measurements

1 metre (m) = 1.09 yards
1 km = 0.621 mile
1 mile = 1.6 km

Contents

Introduction

The walks in this book are all located on the Lizard peninsula. Lizard Point is famous for being the most southerly place in mainland Britain. The peninsula is also famous, the world over, for its natural history. In particular, the Lizard is known for its flowers, which are inextricably linked to its unusual geology, both of which I will refer to frequently in the following pages. Protection of the natural environment of this peninsula is high on the agenda, particularly since the return of the now famous 'Cornish' choughs which breed near the most southerly point. Its geographical location has been critical in defining the Lizard throughout its history, and we can see plenty of evidence of its use through the ages. The Lizard is also one of the most beautiful parts of the county, indeed the world, with its fantastic rugged coastline interspersed with beautiful sandy beaches.

Throughout this book I will refer you to flowers, birds, coastal structures and rocks that might be seen along the way. There are a number of highly significant historical sites within these walks, and many villages and attractions.

In selecting the walks I have used the criteria that I always use for a good walk. Wherever possible they are circular, using paths rather than roads, and include: beautiful scenery; natural history; historical features; other interest; free parking, and somewhere to stop for lunch (café, inn, or at least a beauty spot). Some of the walks haven't satisfied all of these criteria, but only where there are good reasons!

For some of these criteria I have given each walk a 'five-star' rating. Within the text I have highlighted where to park and where you can stop for lunch. For each walk I have provided an overview followed by specific details about the route (in italics), and the points of interest along the way.

The timings given are based on the length of time it took me to complete the walks; these do not include long periods for sitting and looking, so you might need to build in extra time. You might find that I am faster or slower than you but you should be able to use these times as a guide to help you make plans. The distances stated are approximate; within these I have tried to make allowances for the twisting and turning nature of the paths.

The maps are intended as a visual representation of the walk; they are not a substitute for carrying a detailed map. The instructions in the walk description should be enough to get you round, but I recommend that you carry an Ordnance Survey map as well in case you lose the route along the way. All of the walks in this book can be found on the Ordnance Survey Explorer map number 103, The Lizard.

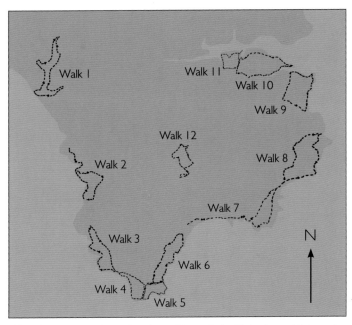

Map showing approximate locations of the walks in this book, roughly to scale

The maps show: the route in a black dashed line with arrows; roads and tracks marked in red (generally, the wider the red line the bigger the road); points of interest marked in blue; start point marked in yellow. Land is green, sea is blue; areas of houses are grey-green. Each has an approximate scale and a north line.

If you are interested in identifying wildlife along the way, you might wish to carry my books *Birds of Cornwall and the Isles of Scilly*, *Wildflowers of Cornwall and the Isles of Scilly*, or *Exploring the Cornish Coast*, all of which are also published by Alison Hodge in the Pocket Cornwall series.

David Chapman, 2014

1 Loe Pool

Beauty	****
Wildlife	*****
Historical interest	****
General interest	****
Distance	10 km (6 miles)
Time	2 hours 45 mins
Walking conditions	Very good, can be muddy in places
Timing	Start 10.30 a.m. for picnic lunch Loe Bar
Start and end point	Free car-park opposite boating lake, Helston (SW 655 271)
Get to to start point	From A394 (bypasses Helston, SW side), turn for Porthleven (B3304) at double roundabout, bottom of Coinagehall Street (main road into town centre); car-park on left after about 180 m
Toilets	Boating lake café

The River Cober near Helston

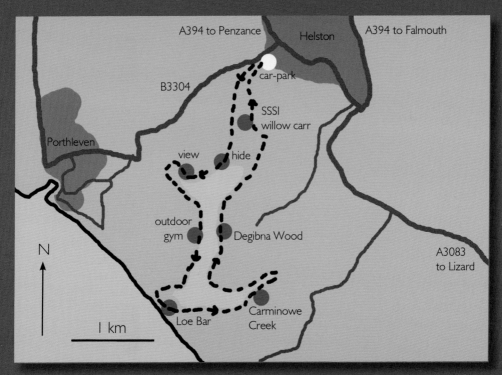

A394 to Penzance
Helston
A394 to Falmouth
car-park
B3304
SSSI
willow carr
Porthleven
view
hide
outdoor
gym
Degibna Wood
N
A3083
to Lizard
1 km
Loe Bar
Carminowe
Creek

Loe Pool is the largest natural lake in Cornwall, and this walk leads around its edge. The walk combines woodland, river, wetland and a dramatic shingle beach as well as the lake and an outdoor gym, should you have energy to burn!

This willow carr is a Site of Special Scientific Interest (SSSI)

The car-park is quite long and there are two footbridges over the river from the car-park. If you park in the first part of the car-park then you will cross the first of the two bridges and turn left on a path. (If it has been very wet it might be wise to turn right along the river for 18 m and then turn left on to the main track to avoid a muddy stretch of path.) Assuming it isn't too wet, continue along the right-hand side of the river, and go past the second footbridge with a pond on your right. A few hundred metres along this path you will come to a T-junction of paths with another footbridge to your left; don't cross the river over this bridge but instead turn right and then shortly turn left on the main track.

Whichever of these two routes you take, you will pass by an area of extremely wet

Clockwise from top left: The main path through woodland along the west side of the valley before you reach the pool; goosanders (these are females) can often be seen in the winter at Loe Pool; bluebells grow beside the path in the Penrose Estate

woodland. This is a Site of Special Scientific Interest (SSSI), packed with lichens and mosses growing on all the trees. Look also at the many ferns, including common polypody which grows on the branches of the more mature trees. In summer there are warblers; in winter you may see kingfishers along the river.

The main track is easy to follow, but it is easy to miss the bird-watching hide down a small path to the left a short distance before a gate and gatehouse.

From the bird-watching hide there are great views over the lake. The best time to look for birds is during the winter when the lake plays host to a wide range of wildfowl including pochard, tufted duck, great crested grebe and goosander; at any time of year there are cormorants, coots and grey herons, and the chance of seeing an otter, though early morning is best for sightings of this elusive creature.

Continue along the main track through the gate and past the gatehouse.

The National Trust offices at Penrose

There is a lovely view from here over the lake, and where the track bends to the right it is always worth stopping to look and listen over the reed-bed. In here, Cetti's warbler sometimes breed, and in cold winters bitterns have been seen. During winter, starlings sometimes roost around the lake (no guarantee!), and this is a good vantage point from which to watch them, but this occurs just after sunset from November to February so will require a special visit.

Turn left at the first junction in the track. This leads across a small river and up towards the old stables of Penrose House where the National Trust (NT) now has its offices.

Where you cross the river, have a look for otter spraint, usually deposited on the top of a rock in or beside the stream. This area of grassland and scattered mature oak trees is known as 'parkland habitat', and is a great place to spot green woodpecker, mistle thrush and buzzard.

Between here and Loe Bar the main track is easy to follow and there is an outdoor gym. By all means try it out, but don't overdo it – you still have most of this walk to complete! 1 hr

The track comes to a more open area which overlooks The Bar.

This spot is a good one for insects. Have a look on the bank to the right of the path, which faces south. Here I have seen small pearl-bordered fritillaries, wall brown butterflies, mining bees and digger wasps in the summer-time.

Continue along the track to the gate and gatehouse, go through the gate and turn back left down to the beach. You are going to cross the beach and head for the edge of the lake to continue the walk, but I advise stopping for a picnic lunch somewhere on The Bar.

This is a barrier beach. The shingle has been forced up against the shoreline since the last Ice Age by rising sea levels, blocking the River Cober to form the lake. The water used to percolate through the shingle but now an outflow has been constructed which keeps it at roughly the same level throughout the year. In hot summers a blue-

green algae can form in the water, so don't allow your dogs to drink from the lake if you are in any doubt.

In summer have a look on the shingle for the unusual flowers that grow here. The most impressive are yellow-horned poppy, sea holly and sea kale. On the bank near the outflow from the lake there are some non-native plants, including Hottentot fig and pampas grass. At any time of year it is worth looking out to sea for seabirds, which always

Loe Bar at sunset (top). Sea holly, Loe Bar (above)

The reed-fringed Loe Pool from the Bar (above).
Memorial to the men of HMS Anson *(left)*

include gannets. On the lake there is usually a good selection of gulls bathing.

In the cliffs at the other side of the bar there is often a colony of sand martins, so look out for these small brown hirundines hunting insects over the lake. You might also like to take a small detour up the coast path

Loe Bar from the south side (left). Lower Pentire, seen across Carminowe Creek (right)

to see the cross of commemoration to the memory of 100 men lost when HMS *Anson* was wrecked on Loe Bar in 1807. This tragedy inspired Henry Trengrouse of Helston to invent a rocket-fired life-saving apparatus which has since saved thousands of lives. 1 hr 20 mins

At the far end of the beach, follow the path beside the lake. For the next couple of miles the path is fairly obvious, just keep turning left wherever there is a choice in paths and keep the lake on your left-hand side.

This arm of the lake is known as Carminowe Creek. It is a slightly more intimate spot, with reeds and trees fringing a narrower section of the lake.

Around the head of the Creek you soon come to the cottages at Lower Pentire. 1 hr 45 mins

The path joins a track, fairly level at first but after about 90 m it bends to the right and starts to climb a hill; just on the bend turn left on to a path through a gap in the hedge (this is easy to miss) to remain on the lake side. Here the path crosses an open field with lovely views over the lake towards The Bar, and soon it heads into Degibna Woods. Follow the main path and keep left where there are any choices, though there are a couple of dead-end paths that lead only to the water's edge.

The unusual evergreen trees here and at other points around the lake are holm oaks. Within Degibna Wood there are many mature trees, and in autumn there is a good selection of fungi; for example, I have found plenty of 'dead-man's fingers' and the aptly-named 'cauliflower fungus'.

A view across Loe Pool from Degibna Wood (above). Dead-man's fingers in the wood (left)

On leaving the woodland the path goes down some steps and then passes by reeds beside the lake. Keep to the lake edge, go through a gate and over a little stream, through a small wood and another gate, and quite soon the path crosses a field. At the end of the field go through a small gate, and after a short distance turn left on to a track by Lower Nansloe

The engine house of Wheal Pool

Farm. This leads back to the car-park where the walk started.

The last stretch of this route leads past the ruined engine house of Wheal Pool mine. This was a lead and silver mine in operation between the sixteenth and nineteenth centuries. In the eighteenth century it produced lead ore which yielded between 30 and 40 ounces of silver per ton – insufficient to give a profit as a silver mine. In the late-eighteenth century an adit was driven through the cliffs at the south end of Loe Pool to lower the level of water to stop the mine flooding. 2 hrs 45 mins

If you would like a cup of tea or a slice of cake to end your walk, then cross the road and visit the café at the other end of the boating lake.

2 Gunwalloe to Mullion Cove

Beauty	*****
Wildlife	***
Historical interest	*****
General interest	*****
Distance	10 km (6 miles)
Time	3 hours
Walking conditions	Fair with some rocky climbs and some steps
Timing	Start 10 a.m. for lunch in Mullion
Start and end point	Car-park at Gunwalloe (NT pay-and-display, charge to non-members)
Get to to start point	From Helston take A3083 on to the Lizard. Pass the main entrance to RNAS Culdrose; about 1 mile further turn right to Gunwalloe (just before a roundabout). Continue through Gunwalloe village and another 2 miles to a large car-park on the left
Toilets	Gunwalloe, Poldhu Cove, Mullion Cove, Mullion

Dollar Cove

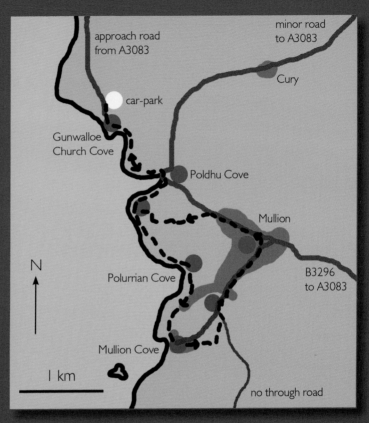

approach road
from A3083

minor road
to A3083

Cury

car-park

Gunwalloe
Church Cove

Poldhu Cove

Mullion

N

Polurrian Cove

B3296
to A3083

Mullion Cove

1 km

no through road

This walk can be done in three hours, but could easily take up a whole day with many points of interest along the way. It takes in four beautiful and varied coves as well as visiting a very unusual church on a beach; the Marconi Centre; Mullion (the highest-populated area on the Lizard), and a chocolate factory with craft centre. There are plenty of options for eating and drinking along the way.

Clockwise from left: The view of Gunwalloe, Church Cove, from the south; Gunwalloe church with its separate tower; an interesting rood screen inside the church

From the car-park cut through at the bottom corner and turn left on to the minor road; soon bear right on a track. Shortly look to the right to see the beautiful and rocky Dollar Cove;

Looking back to Gunwalloe from the headland

a few metres further on, the track ends beside a church in the most remarkable of locations.

Here at Gunwalloe Church Cove there is a small church set at the edge of the beach among the sand dunes, almost hidden from sight. The church was built in the fifteenth century and is unusual not only for its location, but also because it has a tower that is separate from the main church, set into the cliff. The church is dedicated to St Winwaloe, a missionary Breton saint who visited Cornwall sometime during the sixth century. The tower is older than the church – probably thirteenth-century – and may have been part of another building.

Within the church are some interesting items, particularly the well-preserved sections of the rood screen, dating from the early sixteenth century. The carving itself is

After strong westerly winds, check the beaches for goose barnacles

beautiful, but even more significant is the fact that the wood from which it is made was taken from wreckage saved from the *St Antony of Lisbon*, reputedly the King of Portugal's treasure ship, which was wrecked here in 1527.

What this also shows is that this section of coast has a history of wrecks. Perhaps the most famous is the *San Salvador*, a Spanish ship supposedly carrying silver coins which wrecked in Dollar Cove. The silver dollars have attracted interest since 1669 when the ship sank. In recent years divers have explored the site, but in previous centuries people have dug and delved, miners were even said to have sunk a shaft to try to reach the treasure from below!

To continue the walk, cross the beach – the easiest route is at the top of the beach where there is a wooden bridge over the small river.

It is worth exploring the beach for anything interesting washed ashore. After strong westerly winds, this is a good place to find goose barnacles and by-the-wind-sailors.

The coast path up the hill has been diverted recently due to cliff collapses, so please follow all diversions on this walk. The path reaches the top of the hill where there is a small parking area. Continue along the coast path on the north side of Poldhu Cove and down to the beach.

If you are a keen bird watcher, it is worth crossing the road into the car-park at the back of Poldhu beach. Here there is an area of wetland consisting of extensive scrub and reeds, where you may find breeding sedge, reed and Cetti's warbler. In Poldhu Cove, as well as other coves on the west side of the Lizard, you may find colonies of sand martins

The cove and beach at Poldhu (above). Old Poldhu Hotel photographed at sunset (right)

which dig nest holes in the sandy soil at the top of the cliffs. There are a café and toilets at the back of the beach.

Continue on the coast path, which follows the road up the hill on the south side of the Cove. Just before reaching the Old Poldhu Hotel (now a care home), the coast path dips

A view of Polurrian Cove from the south

down to the right. Instead I suggest following the signs to the Marconi Centre, which effectively cuts off this headland going to the left of the Old Hotel. 40 mins

Marconi was responsible for the first radio signal to be transmitted across the Atlantic in 1901, and exactly 100 years later the Marconi Centre was opened at Poldhu to commemorate his momentous achievement. The centre has limited opening times and is staffed by volunteers, so check their website if you wish to visit: www.marconi-centre-poldhu.org.uk. In the field are some aerials used by the Poldhu Amateur Radio Club at exactly the same spot that Marconi used all those years ago.

The Poldhu Hotel was built to accommodate the workers in the wireless station, but one of its most famous guests was Sir Arthur Conan Doyle who wrote one of his stories (The Adventures of the Devil's Foot) while staying here in 1909.

Continue along the coast path southwards to Polurrian Cove. 1 hr

The harbour and boats at Mullion Cove

Polurrian Cove is a popular beach with holiday-makers and surfers. It is actually nearer to Mullion than is Mullion Cove and has a large sandy beach. Geologically, Polurrian is the beginning of the Lizard. All that you have been walking on so far is Devonian slate, laid down at the bottom of a delta some 380 million years ago and since exposed to incredible pressures which have compressed and twisted it. Look back and you will see rocks with layers in them; look ahead and there are none. The rocks which make up the Lizard are mostly serpentine, gabbro and gneiss, and here it is schist. The actual joint, which is visible, is in Polurrian Cove.

Continue along the coast path to Mullion Cove. 1 hr 20 mins

The inlet of Mullion Cove is again a fault between two rock types; here it is between schist and serpentine, which lies ahead on further walks. Mullion Cove has an attractive harbour with two walls and quaint cobbled slipway. It was completed in 1895 by Lord Robartes of Lanhydrock. This cove was

Lobster pots lined up at Mullion Cove

once home to a busy pilchard fishery, and on one of its walls there still remains the old pilchard cellar and net store. It has been used as a location in many films, including *Amazing Grace*, *A Secret to Tell* and *Another View*. From the cove we get a view of Mullion Island, now a bird reserve which supports a population of gulls and a few other seabirds. During summer there is a café open near the cove.

Take the road inland from the cove, up the hill. Soon you pass toilets on the right, and within 50 m turn right on to a footpath that follows a small track up a hill. Near the top of the hill, look for a footpath to the left by a water hydrant. This leads between two hedges, then out on to fields. Stay to the right-hand edge of the fields and soon you reach a minor road. Here turn left. Follow this road to a junction where, on the left, you will see the Chocolate Factory & Craft Centre, which has a café. I hr 40 mins

A view from the path between Mullion Cove and Mullion (left). The church in Mullion (right)

If you don't go to the Chocolate Factory, turn right at the junction and head into Mullion.

Mullion is the largest village on the Lizard, with a population of about 2,300 people. It has a wide range of shops along with some pubs and a fish and chip shop. The church of St Mellanus, in Mullion, has wonderfully carved bench ends depicting scenes from the Bible. Notice also a dog door in the main door (thirteenth-century), which was designed to allow sheep dogs to get in and out freely, much like a modern-day cat flap!

As you enter Mullion you will want to explore the shops, but to continue the walk keep left through the village, passing the church on the right and a lovely small garden with seating suitable for a picnic lunch stop, then at a junction turn left on the road signed to Poldhu and Cury opposite the village car-park. 2 hrs

Continue along this road beyond the end of the village and shortly after passing through the National Speed Limit signs look for a footpath along a track to the left beside the sign for Angrouse Court. Follow this track to its very end which is at the Marconi Centre, then retrace your steps back along the coast. 3 hrs

3 Predannack to Kynance Cove

Beauty	*****
Wildlife	*****
Historical interest	****
General interest	****
Distance	10 km (6 miles)
Time	2 hours 30 mins
Walking conditions	Steep hills; rocky paths close to high cliffs; return can be muddy
Timing	Start 10 a.m. for lunch at Kynance Cove
Start and end point	Car-park Predannack Wollas (NT honesty)
Get to to start point	From Helston take A3083 on to the Lizard. Turn right on B3296 to Mullion. In Mullion turn left; left again, signed to Mullion Cove. After about 1 mile turn left before Chocolate Factory. Road ends in car-park
Toilets	Kynance Cove

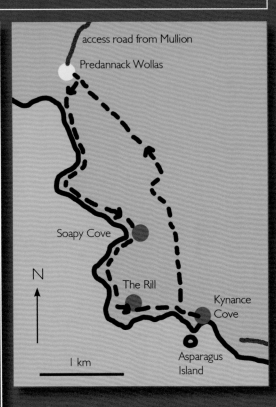

access road from Mullion

Predannack Wollas

Soapy Cove

The Rill

Kynance Cove

Asparagus Island

N

1 km

Wildflowers grow beside the path near Predannack Wollas

This is a remote coastal walk through some little-visited scenery. It is great for botany and bird watching, and climaxes at Kynance Cove where there is a delightful café and wonderful beach. There is also the historic, interesting and aptly named Soapy Cove along the way. (Avoid the inland return route if it has been wet because it can get very muddy.)

Green-winged orchids can be identified by the green veins in the lower petals (left). You may find fringed rupturewort, a very rare plant (above).

host to a wide range of warblers in spring and summer; listen for chiffchaff, whitethroat and even lesser whitethroat.

Continue on the track about another 20 m and turn right on to a footpath signed to the coast path.

Where you turn right on to the path there are some flattish stones on which you might step. Look carefully around these and you may find a very rare plant known as the fringed rupturewort.

Continue along this path and go over a stile.

Around this path, particularly among the rocks to the left, look for green-winged orchids growing among the small outcrops of serpentine rock. These usually flower from late April to mid-May.

Leave the car-park on the track past the honesty box between the farm buildings. Go through the gate and follow the track over a small stream.

In the dip just after the stream there is a lovely area of wildflowers in a small marshy spot. Look for southern marsh orchids here in May/June. The scrubby bushes may play

The cliffs from Vellan Head (above). The peregrine falcon can be seen from the coast path (right)

Continue to the coast path and turn left. You will see a sign to Kynance Cove (2½ miles).

The footpath rises on to an area of heathland high above sea level and quite flat. Many of the clumps of heather here are of Cornish heath. The rock on which you tread throughout this walk is serpentine. The cliffs are high and steep, so be careful if you go near the edge. Look out for peregrine falcons hunt-

Looking down the valley of Soapy Cove

ing along this stretch of coast; these birds of prey have chunky bodies but short, pointed wings and a short tail. They look dark from a distance and fly exceptionally quickly – in fact they are the world's fastest bird. You will also see ravens here, and shags nest on the rocks at the base of the cliffs, so watch out for them flying around at sea.

When approaching Soapy Cove don't try to take a short cut down into the cove, there are old quarries which make this very dangerous. There is a wooden stile over a fence; go over it and down into the valley. You can take a small detour down to the ruined buildings, even down to the beach if you are fit and the tide is out.

This cove is marked on Ordnance Survey maps as Gew-graze, but is known locally as Soapy Cove because of an association with a

Vellan Head seen from Soapy Cove

white rock (steatite) found in the serpentine. This very soft rock – a little like talc – became known as soapstone, and was mined here from the eighteenth century. Soapstone was used in the production of porcelain, but by the early nineteenth century china clay had taken over this purpose, and the quarry at Soapy Cove ceased production. 45 mins

Continue by crossing the small stream and going along the coast path to the south side of the cove.

Look back at the cliffs to see the white soapstone. After about half a mile the path turns along the top of The Rill, with fantastic views over Kynance Cove and Asparagus Island from the top of Kynance Cliff. Here parts of the cliff are steep and very dangerous, but other parts are made of a relatively

Kynance Cove beach from Kynance Cliffs (above). Wild asparagus in flower (left)

gentle slope with boulder scree. Just before a wall it is possible to venture a little way down the slope where you might see a special plant called wild asparagus, after which the island rising from Kynance Cove beach was named.

Pass through this wall, and if you wish to turn back now turn left to head for the gate which is

Kynance Farm is on the return route

visible some 50 m away. Before the gate turn left on to a track.

If you wish to go down to Kynance Cove – which I thoroughly recommend, particularly if you haven't been before or if you want lunch in the café – then continue along the coast path down the hill and return when you have spent some time there. (Add any extra time spent in Kynance to the times given for this walk.)

Kynance Cove, the sea-stacks and islands are made of serpentine – a rock formed some 375 million years ago when a molten intrusion made its way to the earth's surface from the earth's mantle, when it was situated in the Southern hemisphere. Since then it has gradually moved northwards by plate tectonics. About 300 million years ago it was forced on to the rest of what is now Cornwall, and

Clockwise from top left: A fern called pillwort; western gorse; pygmy rush

continued to slide northwards. Serpentine gives rise to very poor soil which isn't suitable for ploughing, so it has been left undisturbed and many wildflowers thrive. 1 hr 20 mins

If you have visited Kynance, then head back up the hill to the wall, turn right before the wall to head for the gate, previously mentioned, then turn left just before the gate on to the track.

In the gateway there is often a very wet patch which is home to a very rare plant called three-lobed water crowfoot.

Continue along this track, which can be quite muddy, and pass through a gate on to a harder track at the top of Soapy Cove valley. Here you will see Kynance Farm. Cross a stream

Left to right: Heather, bell heather and cross-leaved heath

and head up the other side, keeping right. Go through a gate on to a patch of heathland.

This heathland contains heather, bell heather, cross-leaved heath and Cornish heath as well as western gorse, all of which flower in summer. 1 hr 45 mins

Go through a small gate and on to a hard track where you should turn right. Ignore a small path* to the left. Continue to where this track comes to the sign for Predannack Airfield. In front of this sign turn left on a perimeter path. This path can get very muddy.

Predannack Airfield serves as a satellite airfield for RNAS Culdrose and is used mostly by helicopters. Note the mock-ups of helicopters and aircraft which are used for fire practice. At weekends the airfield is used for gliders. It is not accessible to the public. This trackway has some interesting plants growing in the muddy patches. Possibly the most notable are pygmy rush and pillwort, which for botanists are worth looking out for.

Continue until you come to another airfield sign, and then turn left through a small gate. At a junction of footpaths continue straight on (the gate to the left is where the small path* comes in if you choose that to avoid the very muddy conditions of this trackway!). Pass along the edge of a field next to a barbed-wire fence, go over a stile to the right, then bear left to a gate. Pass through a gate, then continue along this track back to the start point. 2 hrs 30 mins

4 Kynance Cove to Lizard Point

Beauty	*****
Wildlife	*****
Historical interest	****
General interest	****
Distance	7 km (4½ miles)
Time	2 hours 30 mins
Walking conditions	Very good, some hilly bits, some bits close to cliff edge
Timing	Start 10.30 a.m. to lunch at café at most southerly point; useful if low tide at start time
Start and end point	NT car-park, Kynance Cove (charge to non-members 10 a.m. to 5 p.m., summer)
Get to to start point	From Helston take A3083 on to the Lizard. Head for Lizard village. Just before village turn right on to minor road signed to Kynance Cove
Toilets	Kynance Cove; Kynance Cove car-park; Lizard Lighthouse; Lizard village

Lizard Point and Pentreath Beach from near Kynance Cove car-park

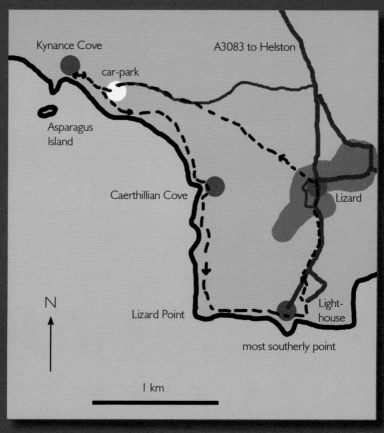

Kynance Cove

A3083 to Helston

car-park

Asparagus Island

Caerthillian Cove

Lizard

N

Lizard Point

Light-house

most southerly point

1 km

This is probably the most popular walk on the Lizard. Kynance Cove is very beautiful, and the walk to Lizard Point is very attractive with lots of wildflower interest. On top of that, you have the chance to sit and eat lunch while watching seals and choughs – all with a great view.

The classic view of Kynance Cove at low tide

From the car-park, walk out on to the cliffs and turn right towards Kynance Cove. This is a slight diversion because we will soon come back to walk the coast path in the other direction! After about 100 m, looking down into the cove you will come across one of the most iconic Cornish views. I suggest it is worth going down to the cove to have a look around.

If you visit in summer, you will find the flowers of bloody cranesbill here. This is a common flower of limestone pavements, but here conditions are suitable because of the high level of magnesium in the serpentine rock on which it grows. Around the top of the steps leading down to the beach is a lovely piece of serpentine showing the rich colours found in it. At low tide you can cross the beach for a coffee in the café before turning round and going back up the coast path.

Back up on top, during spring and summer look for the flowers of spring sandwort, low down among the rocky outcrops. If your visit

Clockwise from top: The beach at Kynance Cove is well worth exploring. Spring sandwort is a very rare flower found on this stretch of coast. Bloody cranesbill growing at Kynance

Left to right: Kidney vetch and thrift grow beside the coast path. Thyme broomrape is a parasitic plant that grows on wild thyme. The flowers of Cornish heath have maroon-coloured rims

is in April or May, you might find early purple orchids on the slopes down to the edge of the cliffs. In May and June there might be thyme broomrape, a parasitic plant with a red stem.

Follow the coast path southwards.

On the high flat ground in this area you will find lots of heathers. The most significant one here is the Cornish heath, endemic to the Lizard; look for the maroon-coloured rim around each little flower. There are plenty of other flowers along here, notably thrift, sea campion, kidney vetch and wild carrot. In summer look for butterflies and moths – the six spot burnet moth is common.

After about a mile the coast path drops down to sea level at Caerthillian Cove. 45 mins

There are two small valleys at Caerthillian. If you walk a few yards up the second valley and look carefully on the slope to your left, you will see that the soil is quite shallow, and there are a lot of very small flowers. This is one of the best places in Britain for clovers. Clovers grow on the infertile ground associated with serpentine because they can fix nitrogen in their root nodes. On this one slope there are eleven different species of clover, most of which flower in summer. You will need a specialist guide to identify the majority of them.

Continue on the coast path, up the hill on the narrow path between two banks.

At the top of this hill you will notice that the vegetation has changed dramatically. No

Caerthillian Cove, a strong wind blowing from the west (above). Choughs are often seen (right)

longer is there any heather, for example. This is because you are no longer on serpentine rock, here it is schist. There aren't quite as many rare flowers now, but it is still possible to find many common species, including autumn squill in late summer. Look out for a friendly kestrel along this stretch of path, and always keep an eye out for the choughs.

Looking back to Kynance from Lizard Point (left).
Hottentot fig growing near Lizard Point (above)

Rounding the corner of Lizard Point we get a view of the most southerly point – our lunch stop.

Just before reaching the most southerly point, look for the unusual flowers on the cliff tops. Here are natives including tree mallow, and non-natives, particularly Hottentot fig and mesembryanthemum. Both are South African in origin; beautiful in flower, they cause damage to our native flora by cloaking the ground with their heavy succulent leaves.

This is a great place to see choughs, and during the summer there is a chough watch point adjacent to Polpeor Café. I recommend eating here, and you might like to buy greetings cards and books from the little shop! You will also see a serpentine shop near the carpark; do have a look in here, and in similar shops in Lizard village. (For more on serpentine and its uses, see Walk 6, pages 52–61.)

While here, walk down the slope towards the old lifeboat house. Polpeor Cove was the site of the Lizard Lifeboat from 1859 to 1959, when it was moved to Kilcobben Cove (see Walk 5, pages 44–51). You might see grey seals, basking on the rocks at low tide or bobbing in the sea at high tide. There will also be shags on the rocks offshore, and a few cormorants. Around the café you might see or hear a small grey-brown bird with a spotted breast and an attractive parachuting display flight: this is a rock pipit. 1 hr 30 mins

The most southerly point seen from Lizard Point

From the most southerly point, don't be tempted to walk up the narrow road; instead, continue a little further on the coast path and take the first left turn to the car-park by the lighthouse. (For more on the lighthouse, see Walk 5, page 46.) Here there are toilets and a well-signed path to Lizard village along the left-hand side of the car-park. In the village, go as far as The Green and turn left just before it. Here you pass more toilets and continue down a minor road. After about 100 m, turn right off the track on to a footpath signed to Kynance Cove. This path leads along the top of a Cornish hedge between two fields, down into a small valley through a lovely woodland, and then up across some damp fields.

In the woodland look for warblers, particularly in spring and summer. In the wet meadow, there are attractive flowers such as ragged robin.

This footpath meets the road on which you drove down to Kynance car-park; turn left on to the road (effectively straight on) and this leads back to the car-park. 2 hrs 30 mins

5 Lizard, Housel Bay, Church Cove

Beauty	*****
Wildlife	***
Historical interest	*****
General interest	*****
Distance	6 km (3½ miles)
Time	1 hour 45 mins
Walking conditions	Very good
Timing	Any time, allow extra time to visit the heritage sites along the way
Start and end point	Lizard Green car-park (honesty box)
Get to to start point	From Helston take A3083 on to the Lizard and continue all the way to Lizard village
Toilets	Adjacent Lizard Green; Lizard Lighthouse

Lizard Lighthouse seen from Pen Olver

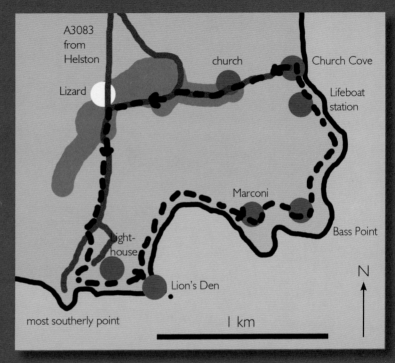

This is a relatively short walk with lots to see and do along the way. Depending on your time of departure, you can eat lunch in Lizard village or at a café at the most southerly point. Highlights include the lighthouse, lifeboat house, church and Marconi's signalling station, but the many coastal features and the chance to see choughs also mean there is a lot packed into this short walk.

(*Note:* The timings do not take into account visiting the heritage sites along the way.)

Lizard Lighthouse

his motives – and the tower was demolished.

In 1751 Thomas Fonnereau erected the twin lighthouse that we see today with a cottage between the two towers. An overseer sat in the cottage and made sure the fires in both towers were kept well alight by the men responsible for pumping the bellows. Trinity House took over responsibility for the lighthouse in 1771; it was electrified in 1924, and automated in 1998.

From Lizard Green take the road towards the most southerly point and use the footpath which runs next to it. This footpath leads into the Lizard Lighthouse car-park. Here you have the opportunity to visit the lighthouse.

The first lighthouse to be built on the headland here was constructed in 1619 by Sir John Killigrew. Some say he was a philanthropic Cornishman, others that he was part of a wrecking family. Though he paid to have it constructed he couldn't afford the upkeep and hoped to take donations from the owners of the ships that passed the Point. Donations were not forthcoming – some say this is because the ship owners were suspicious of

To ensure the lighthouse is open, before you plan your visit please check the Trinity House website (http://www.trinityhouse.co.uk), or phone 01326 290202.

After visiting the lighthouse take the small footpath down the hill past the toilets in the car-park. If you want to eat at the most southerly point, turn right at the bottom of the hill and return afterwards, otherwise turn left. This leads to the headland overlooking Housel Bay.

Along this stretch of coast always keep a look out for adders. Many people spot them here: they like to bask at the edge of coarse vegetation and this area below the lighthouse can be a sun trap.

View across Housel Bay from near Lizard Lighthouse. Notice the blow hole in the foreground

At the first headland you will notice a sea stack and a huge hole, known as a blow hole. These blow holes are formed when a cave develops so far inland under the ground that the weight of the land forces a collapse. The collapse of this blow hole took place on the night of 19 February 1847. The Victorians had romantic notions about these coastal features, and named this one The Lion's Den. Be very careful because this is an unstable feature and is not fenced.

Continue along the coast path around Housel Bay. After about half a mile the path dips down into a small valley. At this point there is the option to take a small diversion to the right down into Housel Cove beach – at low tide the

beach is delightful and well worth the extra few metres. The main path takes a turn to the left, and then you must shortly turn right to continue along the coast path. This leads in front of the Housel Bay Hotel and out towards Pen Olver headland.

Watch out for choughs along this stretch... in fact it is easier to listen for their 'chiow' calls as you will need to keep your eyes firmly fixed on the path ahead.

In 1900 Guglielmo Marconi stayed at the Housel Bay Hotel and leased a plot of land in an adjacent wheat field. Here he built the Lizard Wireless Telegraph Station, which still stands, recently renovated by the NT. The main purpose of this station was to communicate with passing ships and to act as a monitoring station for the trans-Atlantic station at Poldhu. In 1910 the station was the first to receive an

Housel Cove, from rocks near the beach (top). Lizard Lighthouse seen from near Housel Bay Hotel (above)

SOS message from a ship, the *Minnehaha*, which interestingly was two years before the *Titanic* disaster. This signal station is owned by the NT and leased to the Trevithick Trust. It is found in a wooden hut just inland of the coast path, and is open some afternoons in the summer. It is best to check before visiting, by phoning 01326 561407, or visiting www.lizardwireless.org.

The Lloyds Signal Station, built in 1872, was used to communicate to passing ships with flags and flares, though it later operated using wireless systems and was owned by Lloyds of London from 1883 to 1951.

Continuing along the coast path, we soon come to Bass Point where there is a voluntary coastguard building.

National Coastwatch Institution (NCI) manages the lookout at Bass Point. This building had lain dormant until 1994 when two local fishermen lost their lives within sight of this, then empty, lookout. Locals decided to set up an organization to restore watches around the coast of the UK, and so the NCI was born. The first station to open was this one at Bass Point in December 1994. 1 hr

After Bass Point follow the track but shortly turn right on to the coast path. Continue along the coast path until you come to the Lifeboat station.

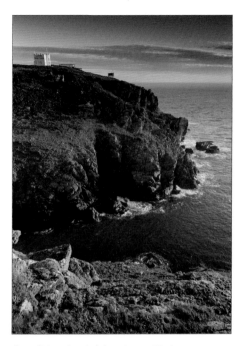

Bass Point, the signal station and lookout, seen from Pen Olver

The first lifeboat station around Lizard Point was at Polpeor Cove, near the most southerly point (see Walk 4, pages 36–43). That one was built in 1859, but in 1959 a new one was built here at Kilcobben Cove. In 2012, this was superseded by a newer lifeboat house, designed to house a Tamar class

Clockwise from top left: The old lifeboat house; the new lifeboat house; the view along the east coast of the Lizard from near the lifeboat house

boat, located down 200 steps and built at a cost of £7.4 million. (At the time of writing, the lifeboat station is open Monday to Thursday 10.30–15.30; Friday 10.30–12.30, and weekends 12.00–16.00.)

Continue on the coast path, which leads off down the side of the lifeboat station building at the top of the cliff. Follow this as far as Church Cove and then turn left on the minor road as far as Lizard village, past the church of St Wynwallow.

Although the village is called Lizard, it belongs to the parish known as Landewednack. It is likely that this church was founded as the daughter church of the abbey of Landevennec in Brittany, France. The parish church is dedicated to St Wynwallow. It is a Grade II listed building, the oldest part of which is the Norman doorway; the rest of the church is fifteenth-century.

Continue straight on up the road. This leads back to the start point. 1 hr 45 mins

The view walking down towards Church Cove (top). The church of St Wynwallow (above)

6 Lizard to Poltesco and Cadgwith

Beauty	****
Wildlife	***
Historical interest	*****
General interest	*****
Distance	12 km (7½ miles)
Time	3 hours 30 mins
Walking conditions	Quite a lot of ups and downs on coast path, muddy in places
Timing	Start at 9.30 a.m. for lunch in Cadgwith on way back
Start and end point	Lizard Green car-park (honesty box)
Get to to start point	From Helston take A3083 on to the Lizard and continue to Lizard village
Toilets	Lizard Green; Cadgwith

The first view of Cadgwith on the coast path from Poltesco

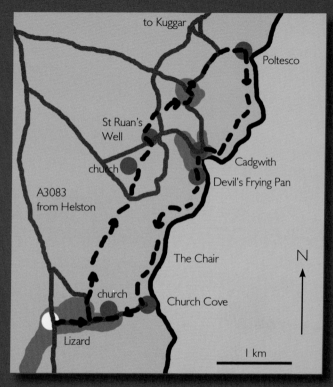

to Kuggar

Poltesco

St Ruan's
Well

church

Cadgwith

Devil's Frying Pan

A3083
from Helston

The Chair

N

church

Church Cove

Lizard

1 km

This is a highly recommended walk calling in at three very pretty coves including the well-known Cadgwith Cove, complete with pub and fishing boats, and the much less well-known Poltesco, site of a disused pilchard fishery and serpentine factory. There are plenty of cracking views along a very attrac-tive, rugged stretch of coastline, and don't overlook this interesting inland route. I have designed the walk to pass through Cadgwith, so you can choose to have lunch on the re-turn leg. Alternatively, take a packed lunch to eat at the walk's climax at Poltesco.

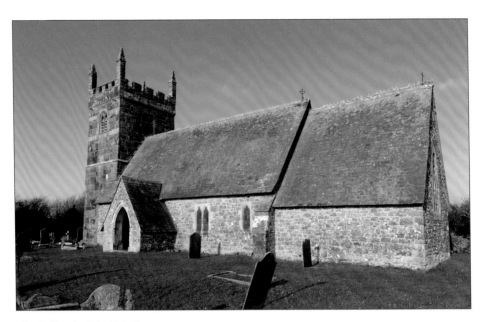

Grade Church of the Holy Cross

Start from Lizard Green and take the road signed to Church Cove (Beacon Terrace). After about 500 m the road bends left by a cross.

This Celtic cross is now very worn, but clearly it once had a plain, straight-armed cross on its head and the lower part continued down to the ground. It is thought that these crosses might have marked religious routes, and may have been places at which prayers were offered. This cross was moved after the Second World War.

Continue along the road (signed to Helston) and turn right (effectively straight on) where the road again bends left, climbing over a stile beside a gate, on a footpath signed to Cadgwith. Soon you come to two gates with a stile between; take the stile and follow the next field along its left-hand side.

Head for Trethvas farmhouse, and when you come to a stile and gate climb the stile and turn left on the track towards the house. In front of the farmhouse turn right on the footpath signed to Cadgwith and Ruan Minor.

Ahead, to the left of a gate, is a stile which takes you on to a footpath along the top of a hedgebank. Continue along here until another stile leads down and the path then crosses a small field and into a copse. At the minor road turn right. 30 mins

After a few metres, turn left on to a footpath opposite Gwavas Jersey Farm, through the gate of Gwavas Vean. Keep left of Gwavas Vean and go over stiles beside a gate. Once into this field, initially stay to the right-hand side, but you can see a church – Grade Church of the Holy Cross – and can cross the field to get there.

This church is dedicated to St Grada. It has medieval origins, but though the tower is old the rest of the building dates from 1862. In the thirteenth century, the parish was known as St Cross, but since the fourteenth century it became known as St Grada, Virgin. In 1934 the hamlets of Grade, Ruan Major and Ruan Minor were united into the single parish of Grade Ruan.

After a look around this interesting church, come back into the same field and stay to the left-hand edge. Soon take the stile to the left,

St Ruan's Well

and then aim straight across the middle of this field, just to the left of the distant Methodist Church in Ruan Minor. At the hedge there is another stile; go over this and straight across the minor road to come face-to-face with St Ruan's Well.

Clockwise from left: The stream at Poltesco Mill; the pilchard and serpentine processing buildings at Poltesco, Carleon Cove; a view towards Black Head from the coast path near Poltesco

It is thought that this well dates to the fifteenth century and was restored in the nineteenth century. It is remarkable in being beautifully faced with stone, and has a round-arched opening and pitched roof.

From the well, cross the field to a stile and turn right on the farm road. Shortly turn right on to a track marked 'footpath' just before a house named Lyndale. Go over a stile and cross the field aiming for the nearest houses. Go over the stile and between the houses to a minor road; turn right here. 1 hr

This minor road soon bends to the right; take a footpath to the left here, and soon the foot-

Cadgwith Cove with its fishing boats hauled out on to the beach

path heads up a track to the right. This comes out on to a minor road; go straight up the road to the junction beside the Methodist church. Turn left on this road in Ruan Minor. The road bends to the left; immediately after the primary school turn right on to a very minor road beside the school. Continue down this road until it crosses a stream beside Poltesco Mill House. As you start up the other side there is a junction; turn right here and then right again on to a footpath which crosses a bridge over the stream again. (This footpath is signed to Carleon Cove.) Shortly there is another right turn on to a footpath, again signed to Carleon Cove.

This footpath meets the coast path and you will go straight on, heading south along the

Looking back to Cadgwith from the coast path south of the village

coast path, but first you will want to go down to the Cove to look at the ruined buildings and beautiful beach. 1 hr 30 mins

The ruined buildings at Poltesco (the hamlet around Carleon Cove) were once used for two purposes: packing pilchards and polishing serpentine. Pilchards used to be very numerous around the coast of Cornwall, particularly in summer. Sometimes huge shoals of fish would come towards the shore, and along the coast 'huers' were positioned to spot them; alert the men on the fishing boats with their cries, and guide the nets into position by a sort of semaphore system. Such was the importance of this work that at various points around the coast of Cornwall, huers' huts can still be seen.

The story of serpentine in Poltesco began in 1855, and was spurred on by the interest shown by Queen Victoria. Serpentine be-

The cove of Polgwidden, south of Cadgwith

came a highly fashionable product after the Queen and Prince Albert were presented with serpentine vases during a visit to Cornwall in 1846, and later used the stone at Osborne House. For a time serpentine was in huge demand as houses throughout the world installed pillars, fireplaces and other accessories. Factories such as the Lizard Serpentine Factory at Poltesco worked flat out producing architectural pieces. The stone,

beautifully patterned in red or green, must have looked spectacular, but sadly it proved a poor interior investment because it dries out and cracks when subjected to dry heat, so the fireplaces sent to hot climates – India, for example – soon began to crumble. That and changing fashions led to the demise of the industry and the loss of the factory in 1893. It is still possible to see some of the work from Poltesco, however, because the pulpit at St

The Devil's Frying Pan, near Cadgwith

buildings that you can see today are, on the left, the warehouse and showroom of the serpentine factory, and, on the right, the capstan house belonging to the pilchard fishery.

After looking at the cove and buildings, go back to the coast path; turn left, going south towards Cadgwith. The route is now easy to follow.

On the way down to Cadgwith you will pass a hut with a bench. The hut was built as a coastguard lookout in the nineteenth century, and subsequently was used as a huer's hut. Cadgwith was once a very busy fishing cove; in fact it holds the record for the number of pilchards caught in one day – a staggering 1.3 million in a single day in the nineteenth century! It is still a fishing cove, and one of the most attractive of such villages in Cornwall. There are places to eat in Cadgwith, or to sit and enjoy a picnic before moving on. 2 hrs 15 mins

Take the road out of the village to the south, up a steep, short hill and at the first bend take the coast path to the left. This path now climbs steeply and is well signed to the coast path and the Devil's Frying Pan.

The Devil's Frying Pan is a collapsed sea cave, this one much more advanced than the Lion's Den on Lizard Point (page 47). The arch at its entrance will one day collapse, leading to the creation of a new cove.

Peter's church in Coverack is made from serpentine and was donated by the company (see Walk 7, pages 66 and 68).

By the early twentieth century, the two big industries that had once excited Poltesco were closing and Carleon Cove was becoming a shadow of its former self. The main

Boats hauled out at Church Cove

Continue along the coast path to the minor road at Church Cove. 3 hrs 10 mins

Here you will turn right up the road back to the starting point, but first turn left to explore this cove. Notice the old lifeboat station, and the many small boats which still use the cove and are winched back up the beach. The return road takes you up a valley past some attractive thatched cottages and past the church (see Walk 5, pages 44–51). 3 hrs 30 mins

7 Kennack Sands to Coverack

Beauty	*****
Wildlife	****
Historical interest	****
General interest	****
Distance	15 km (9½ miles)
Time	4 hours 30 mins
Walking conditions	Quite a lot of ups and downs on coast path; can be wet; rocks can be polished and slippery
Timing	Start at 9.30 a.m. for lunch in Coverack
Start and end point	Kennack Sands (pay car-park)
Get to to start point	From Helston take A3083 on to the Lizard. Just after RNAS Culdrose turn left at roundabout, signed to St Keverne (B3293). Turn right at next roundabout. About 1 mile after Goonhilly Satellite Earth Station turn right, signed to Kuggar. Give way in Kuggar and turn left, signed to Kennack Sands. Road ends in car-park (or park carefully by roadside)
Toilets	Kennack Sands; Coverack

There is a sculpture park along this walk

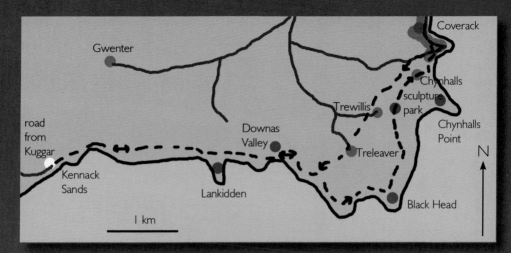

This is a beautiful walk with lots of wildlife interest. It climaxes in the pretty village of Coverack for lunch, and even passes through a sculpture park *en route*. It traverses some of the least visited stretches of the coast path on the Lizard. Do this walk in June to see bloody cranesbill in flower and the best chance of a basking shark, or try August for the best display of Cornish heath.

Butcher's broom – an unusual shrub at Kennack Sands (left). The Sands seen from the west end (right)

From the car-park, take the coast path to the east, which leads slightly uphill past the toilets. Alternatively, if the tide isn't high it should be possible to cross the beach and then climb over the dunes on the first small headland.

This is an interesting area for natural history, with a lot of one particular type of bush known as 'butcher's broom', which has large red berries in autumn. Look for a wide range of flowers here, and a kestrel is frequent. Nesting in the sandy cliffs of the second bay there is usually a colony of sand martins; on the rocks at the back of the beach there are many common lizards, particularly in late summer; the stream and pools play host to many dragonflies.

Continue along the coast path which leads up a steep hill through gorse and heathland. This affords great views back over Kennack Sands.

Anywhere from here to the end of the walk, look out for Cornish heath (a rare type of heather, endemic to the Lizard) and bloody cranesbill. There are also heath spotted orchids at various points on the way. Along this first stretch on the high ground, listen and watch out for a Dartford warbler (a rare resident species). The bay at Kennack

Sands, and along towards Black Head, often attracts basking sharks in summer.

The first point of historical interest is at Lankidden, a promontory with an obvious bank and ditch across its narrow neck. This is what remains of an Iron Age cliff castle. It is estimated that the ditch is about 2 m deep; the bank rises to 4 m, and the whole rampart is about 100 m long. 1 hr

Continue along the coast path, which soon dips down into the attractive Downas Valley, where there is a stream and at low tide a sandy beach.

This is a lovely spot to stop and enjoy a drink while looking for birds. On one visit I saw peregrine, raven, kestrel and stonechat.

Continuing along the coast path we soon come to Black Head. 1 hr 30 mins

Not far along the coast path from Black Head there

Looking back to Kennack Sands from Eastern Cliff (top). Embankment defence of the Iron Age cliff castle at Lankidden (above)

Bloody cranesbill at Treleaver Cliffs, with Nankidden in the distance

at Chynhalls hamlet. *Turn left here, and then almost immediately turn right on to a footpath down a hill; then on the road turn right into the village.*

There are plenty of places to eat and rest here. My walk ends at the church of St Peter, on the sea front, which has a pulpit made of serpentine from the nearby Poltesco factory (see Walk 6, pages 52–61). In the village, the Paris Hotel is named after an American ship wrecked in May 1899 with 700 passengers on board, all of whom were rescued. 2 hrs 45 mins

My return route is inland. It isn't particularly interesting, but it does cut off some distance and saves time; if you have plenty of time you might prefer to return by the coastal path. From the church head back along the road and turn right on the second footpath, between two thatched cottages and up between houses on a surfaced path. This goes up a steep hill and joins a road; turn right here and climb steeply until you go past a school on the right. After the school, the road bends sharply right, but take the footpath which goes straight on here.

is an alternative route inland of the main coast path; in my opinion, it is worth taking this. It is much less rocky and circuitous than the coast path, and it passes by a rather interesting sculpture park. So where the official coast path turns right off the path, continue straight on.

The sculpture park contains work by Terence Coventry, an ex-farmer; the park is free to enter and is in a very attractive setting. The only drawback with this route is that you miss Chynhalls Point, which has the ruins of another Iron Age fort, but the route into Coverack is most appealing.

Pass through the sculpture park on the public footpath and you will come to a minor road

Chynhalls Point from Black Head

Follow the left-hand side of the first field; go over a stile, then after a few metres look for the stile in the hedge to the left; cross through here (it is quite a difficult stile). Go diagonally across the middle of this field and over another difficult stile through a hedge. Follow the right-hand side of this field and look for a stile in the hedge facing you. Now head for the right-hand side of the barn ahead, climb over the stile here

and on to a farm road. Turn left and then soon turn right where the footpath is signed (before Ebber Cottage), along another farm road.

This soon meets a minor road. Turn left and immediately right on to a footpath over a stile (opposite Trewillis Farm). Walk straight across the field following the row of telegraph poles, over a stile and across the middle of the next field to a stile by a gate. Pass through here,

Coverack: harbour and beach (above); St Peter's Church (left). Facing: The beach (top) and harbour (below)

turn right and then immediately left on to a minor road. Soon you come to a small NT car-park; bear right here on a track. Go past Pedna Boar Bungalow, and bear left on to a smaller track. This path leads through a small gate by the NT sign for Beagles Point. 3 hrs 30 mins

Soon this path joins the cost path again; turn right here and retrace your steps back to Kennack Sands. 4 hrs 30 mins

8 St Keverne to Porthoustock and Coverack

Beauty	*****
Wildlife	****
Historical interest	*****
General interest	*****
Distance	13 km (8½ miles)
Time	3 hours 15 mins
Walking conditions	Numerous ups and downs on coast path; very wet section on coast path near Coverack
Timing	Start at 9.30 a.m. for lunch in Coverack
Start and end point	St Keverne free parking in square or on roadside (or park in Coverack and follow directions in text from there)
Get to to start point	From Helston take A3083 on to the Lizard. Just after RNAS Culdrose turn left at roundabout, signed to St Keverne (B3293). Turn right at next roundabout; continue to St Keverne and park
Toilets	St Keverne, Coverack, Porthoustock

The square in St Keverne

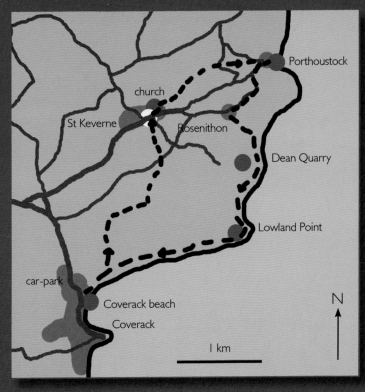

church

Porthoustock

St Keverne

Rosenithon

Dean Quarry

Lowland Point

car-park

Coverack beach

Coverack

N

1 km

This is a very varied walk, full of surprises and interest along the way. The inland sections lead through some idyllic woodland and small hamlets. The coast has several very beautiful coves and a great deal of geological and geomorphological interest, with evidence of sea-level change around Lowland Point. Our exploitation of the local geology is also much in evidence, with quarries and jetties very much a part of the route which takes in two quite contrasting coastal villages. The climax of the walk is in Coverack, where cafés and pubs provide plenty of lunch opportunities.

Lesser celandines grow in the wooded valley between St Keverne and Porthoustock

The footpath from St Keverne leads through the churchyard. Do look in this fine church, whose spire is so tall that it is used by mariners to help them round The Manacles — a reef out at sea. (The name derives from Cornish *Maen eglos* = 'stones of the church'.)

Go through two kissing gates at the far side of the churchyard; then follow the left-hand side of this field at first. The path cuts through the hedge to the left, then continues along the right-hand side of the field; soon cross two stiles and a track and follow the path straight ahead. The path continues along the left-hand side of a field before entering a beautiful woodland.*

In spring this wood has lots of flowers, including bluebells, primroses, wood sorrel, lesser celandine, opposite-leaved golden saxifrage and dog violets. There are the tracks of badgers, lots of birds, and the oil beetle also occurs here.

Porthoustock: beach (above) and village (right)

The footpath soon crosses the stream. Notice non-native gunnera and bamboo here. Follow the valley bottom to a minor road, turn left, then just after the house on the left turn right on to a footpath. Continue on this path down the left-hand side of the valley to emerge on to a road in Porthoustock. Turn right and go down to the centre of the village. 30 mins

You will probably want to wander and explore the beach. Some fishing boats operate

Godrevy Cove

Turn left in Rosenithon by the post box, signed to 'coast path'. Go down to the stream and turn left through the kissing gate. Follow this path to the beach at Godrevy Cove. You are now on the coast path proper and will follow the coast to Coverack. 1 hr

The beach at Godrevy Cove is very picturesque and interesting for wildlife. There are lots of flowers on the dunes, including wild carrot, thrift, kidney vetch, sea campion and sea sandwort to name but a few. At sea look for grey seals and shags, while on the rocks around the beach you may see basking common lizards.

The coast path soon passes by Dean Quarry. This is a gabbro quarry used off and on since the 1890s. Gabbro is used as a road stone in tarmac. On site the rock is crushed and graded, then shipped out from the nearby jetty. You can see the grading storage bays as you walk by. Look for the distinctive field horsetails in the viewing area for the quarry.

After the quarry we soon come to Lowland Point – a raised beach, formed when sea levels were much higher than they are today. We can recognize this because it is a flat area

from here but the beach is dominated by the old jetty and mill building. The disused mill once crushed stone from the nearby quarries.

On the road, cross the small stream and follow the coast path sign – 'Coverack, 3½ miles'. This leads up out of the village and a little inland, avoiding the quarries. At the first road junction turn left, signed 'coast path'. Go up a short stretch of road and turn right over a stile, again signed 'coast path'. Cross the field diagonally (to the left); in the next field go in the same direction; in the third field cross to the left; go through the stile by the gate on to the minor road. Turn right here and walk to the hamlet of Rosenithon (= 'nest in the moors'.)

Clockwise from top: Dean Quarry; Dean Quarry jetty (view north); Dean Quarry jetty and the view towards Lowland Point

adjacent to the sea, and if you look inland you will see an escarpment of rock that was a sea cliff line at a time when sea levels were much higher. The current beaches of large rounded boulders are known as storm beaches because the sea, when it is very rough, can throw these boulders high up the beach.

After Lowland Point keep close to the edge and you may spot the remains of a salt works which was used some 1,800 years ago. Salt water was boiled in clay troughs until the water evaporated, leaving a residue of salt.

The next stretch of path can be very muddy, so take care. Near Coverack the path joins a gravelled track at the top of a hill; here look for a footpath sign to the right: 'to St Keverne via Trevalsoe, 1½ miles'. This will be your return route, but go straight on to explore Coverack.

In Coverack it is well worth looking at the interpretation panel at the foot of the car-park. This explains the significance of the geology to be seen on the beach. 2 hrs 15 mins

When you are ready to retrace your steps, head north along the sea front and turn right on the minor road signed on the coast path to 'Porthoustock, 3½ miles'. Where the surface of

From top: Storm beach, Lowland Point; Ram, or Head, near Lowland Point; raised beach at Lowland Point, looking towards Coverack

Coverack beach

this road changes from tarmac to gravel turn left on to the footpath signed to St Keverne.

The path is quite easy to follow, twisting through woodland, small fields and a kissing gate. Bear left after this and follow the main path. Soon bear right to a gate; go through it and cross the next field. Climb the stile by the next gate and turn right on the farm track. Go along the track in front of the houses and bear right on to the footpath. Soon you come to another minor road; turn right here to Trevalsoe.

This road ends in the hamlet and you will see ahead two footpaths; take the one to the left before the hedgebank. Cross the small field, through a stile then bear right aiming towards the distant spire of St Keverne Church.

Go over a stile and along the right-hand side of a field; over another stile and then follow the path between two hedges. Cross another stile and then follow the path across the middle of the field ahead. Then you come to a stile and a road; cross the road and continue straight ahead. This path leads directly to St Keverne. Where you come to a minor road, just keep straight ahead. 3 hrs 15 mins

9 Porthallow to Nare Point

Beauty	****
Wildlife	***
Historical interest	****
General interest	****
Distance	7 km (4½ miles)
Time	2 hours
Walking conditions	Quite easy going
Timing	Start at 10 a.m. to return to Porthallow for lunch, or take a picnic
Start and end point	Porthallow Beach car-park (honesty box)
Get to to start point	From Helston take A3083 on to the Lizard. Just after RNAS Culdrose turn left at roundabout, signed to St Keverne (B3293). Turn right at next roundabout. Continue to St Keverne; turn left in the square, then follow signs to Porthallow. Park on the beach
Toilets	Porthallow

Boats hauled out at Porthallow

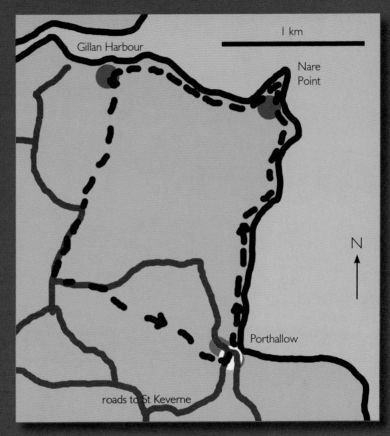

Gillan Harbour

Nare Point

1 km

N

Porthallow

roads to St Keverne

This is a short walk offering great views along the coast as far as Dodman Point. The panorama from Nare Point is particularly beautiful. Although there isn't a suitable café at the half-way point, there is a lovely picnic spot at The Herra, near Gillan, or you might want to start early enough to get back to the pub in Porthallow for lunch.

The beach at Porthallow (above). On the coast path near Porthallow (left)

The route from Porthallow heads north along the back of the beach past the modern and attractive village hall. Notice the rather amusing weather-forecasting stone on the house just before the steps. From here, just follow the coast path sign as far as Nare Point.

Along the way watch out for whitethroats if you do this walk in spring or early summer.

First view of Nare Point from the coast path (above). Looking from Nare Point into the mouth of the Helford (right)

There are lots of spring flowers, and the blackthorn blossom combines to great effect with gorse flowers in April. 40 mins

It isn't a long walk to Nare Point, a significant spot as it is situated at the seaward end of the River Helford on the south side. It is a valued area for wildlife with very interesting

Down on the beach at Parbean Cove (above).
The NCI building at Nare Point (left)

rock pools; offshore lie large beds of maerl – a rare form of calcified seaweed that offers protection to an abundance of marine life.

The headland is obviously of strategic importance. During the Second World War it was mocked up as a decoy for Falmouth Docks to confuse the German bombers. Elaborate lighting was set up to achieve this.

The path leading from Nare Point towards Gillan Creek

The Ministry of Defence observation post was used from 1952 to 1993 as part of a torpedo-testing programme. This building has been taken on by the NCI since 2007.

Several ships have foundered on the rocks close by, one of the more recent ones being in 1920 when the *Rock Island Bridge* hit another ship off Lizard. She was towed to the mouth of the Helford where she listed and sank. Explosives were used to reduce her, and she has since become a popular dive site and a valuable habitat for marine life.

Standing on Nare Point you get a good view. From the left you will see: Gillan Creek and Dennis Head (see Walk 10, pages 86–95); the Helford River along which you should be able to make out the beach at Trebah Garden and the hamlet of Durgan; slightly further on is Rosemullion Head, then Falmouth. Across the Carrick Roads from Falmouth you will see St Mawes, then the lighthouse at St Anthony Head, on the Roseland Peninsula; after that, the island is Gull Rock, and the distant headland is Dodman Point.

The small quay near Gillan, known as The Herra

From the NCI building follow the track around the lower side of the headland towards Gillan Creek. When you pass through a gate, take the path to the right to stay along the shoreline. The path will take you through the NT property of Trewarnevas Cliff, which looks lovely in spring with bluebells, primroses and blackthorn. When you come to the tall pine and fir trees, take the steps down to the right, which emerge on to the small quay known as The Herra, near the hamlet of Gillan. Stop here for a while to explore and maybe have lunch; it's a beautiful, tranquil spot. 1 hr 5 mins

From the quay take the path directly inland up the left-hand side of the valley. When you go through a gate turn right on to a farm track

The attractive valley path leading back down to Porthallow

and follow it through the farm and as far as a crossroads. Here go straight on. Follow this minor road for about 500 m, then turn left on to another minor road signed to 'Porthallow 1¼ miles'. About 500 m along this road, take the footpath to the right opposite The Cider House.

This footpath leads along a small track and over a little stream into a pretty bluebell wood.

It then continues down the right-hand side of a small, attractive valley until it emerges at Porthallow. Turn left on the road to get back to the car-park. 2 hrs

10 Helford to St Anthony-in-Meneague

Beauty	*****
Wildlife	****
Historical interest	***
General interest	***
Distance	9 km (5½ miles)
Time	2 hours 45 mins
Walking conditions	Easy, partly on small, but attractive, road
Timing	Start at 11 a.m. to eat packed lunch on Dennis Head, or 10 a.m. to eat in café at Manaccan, or in public house or café on return to Helford (café in Helford car-park open Easter to October half-term; pub in Helford open all year)
Start and end point	Helford pay-and-display car-park
Get to to start point	From Helston take A3083 on to the Lizard. Just after RNAS Culdrose turn left at roundabout, signed to St Keverne (B3293). Turn right at next roundabout; continue through Garras; after a further 1 mile turn left, signed to Manaccan. At T-junction in Newtown-in-St Martin turn right, then immediately left, signed to Manaccan. After a further 3 miles turn left, signed to Helford. Car-park on right before village
Toilets	Car-park at Helford

Little egrets are often numerous in Gillan Creek

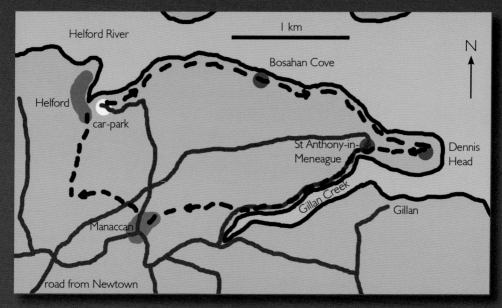

Helford River

1 km

Bosahan Cove

N

Helford

car-park

St Anthony-in-
Meneague

Dennis
Head

Gillan Creek

Gillan

Manaccan

road from Newtown

This is one of the more sheltered walks on the Lizard, following the course of the Helford River and Gillan Creek through attractive woodland. It is a good choice on a windy day! Visit in spring to see the beautiful woodland flowers at their best, or in autumn/winter to see the largest numbers of wading birds on the creeks. This and Walk 11 (pages 96–103) are relatively short, so can be combined into one long walk split by lunch in Helford if you have time.

Wild garlic along the path from the car-park

Near the entrance to the car-park, take the coast path which runs between the road and the car-park in the direction of the yacht club. In spring there is a lovely display of wild garlic (ramsons) along this footpath.

The footpath meets a small road. It is worth taking a little detour to the left to look at Treath Quay and the views back to Helford, and over to Helford Passage.

Among the people of Treath, which is one of the oldest settlements of the Helford area, there is a tradition of 'trigging' – collecting cockles from the shore on Good Friday.

Go back up the small road, just past the footpath you came down, and take the left turning where there is a coast path sign. Shortly you will come alongside the Bosahan Estate, and the path meanders through woodland beside the Helford River. Listen out for birds in this woodland, particularly tits and goldcrests.

The view of Helford from Treath Quay

This path doesn't go past the entrance to Bosahan Garden, so if you want to visit you will need to make a diversion – and make sure first that the gardens are open (phone 01326 231351). Generally, they are open on weekdays during the summer. Compared with many other Cornish gardens, Bosahan is less well known and less developed, so it offers a slightly different experience.

From the first beach you get a good view back over the Helford to (from the left) Trebah Garden, Durgan, Porth Saxon and Toll Point.

Keep along the coast path through a patch of hydrangeas, which are part of Bosahan Garden. The second beach, called Bosahan Beach, has a boathouse. 30 mins

At the next cove (Pensence Cove) keep left close to the edge of the river. The path soon leaves the woodland and follows the left-hand edge of some fields. The view ahead is of the

Helford Passage seen across the River Helford (left). Durgan from the walk (right)

village of Gillan, while to the left you can now see St Anthony Lighthouse and St Mawes (on the opposite side of the Carrick Roads).

Go on to the headland, to a kissing gate. 1 hr

Turn left here for a lovely viewpoint with a bench (a good place for lunch if you like), then go back and through the kissing gate. From here, the quick route is straight down across this field, bearing right to a gate, but it's worth walking round a small circular path to the tip of Dennis Head. To do this, turn left after the kissing gate, then turn left over a stile.

The correct name for Dennis Head is Dinas Head. *Dinas* means a cliff castle or hill fort, and is applied in many other Cornish place-names, including Castle-an-Dinas (hill

The view from Dennis Head to (left to right) Rosemullion Head, St Anthony Lighthouse and Dodman Point

forts near Crowlas and Goss Moor) and Tre-ryn Dinas (a cliff castle near Treen). You will notice earth works here which are thought to be ancient defences, possibly of Celtic origin, but also used by Royalists in the Civil War. In fact, this was one of the last places to surrender, with only Pendennis Castle and St Michael's Mount holding out for longer.

Here you can't get lost, but the path will bring you back to the same stile. So come back over the stile, turn right and go back to near the kissing gate before turning left to follow the path down the field and to the gate into St Anthony. Turn left on the small road and have a look around the church and little hamlet.

St Anthony church seen from a boat trip

Stories suggest that this church was built by a band of shipwrecked Normans who vowed that if they were saved from the tumultuous seas they would build a church dedicated to St Anthony wherever they landed. Since this church is made of a fine-grained granite, unknown to Cornwall but found in Normandy, there may be some truth in this story.

The first mention of this church in a document comes from AD 1170, and the church was rebuilt in the twelfth century. The chancel and south part of the nave date back to that period, and the old font can be seen beside the later, fifteenth-century font in the church. During the fifteenth century, much of the church was enlarged, and further developments have occurred through the years. Inside the church, visitors can buy a fascinat-

Looking up Gillan Creek to the hamlet of Carne

ing booklet detailing its history. Please pause and buy a copy to help maintain the church for future generations.

Then continue along the road with the creek on your left-hand side.

This is an attractive road with good views of Gillan Creek and its bird life. Look for little egrets, grey herons and a variety of other wading birds which might include dunlin, redshank, greenshank and common sandpiper, depending upon the time of year.

Unless you want to look around, don't go down the steps to the left where there is a sign to the stepping stones. A little further along the road on the left there is an optional footpath, which wanders through the woodland, coming back to the road further along. 1 hr 40 mins

Manaccan. Note the 200-year-old fig tree that is growing from the wall of the church (right)

The road dips down very close to the creek at a very beautiful spot. Soon after this there is a footpath to the right, which cuts steeply back to the right and goes up a hill through a gate; look for the footpath sign. The path then continues uphill and bends around to the left. It soon passes through the hamlet of Roscaddon and straight on it passes Manaccan cemetery, where there are several yew trees. Soon you will come to the pretty church, worth a look inside. Go straight through the churchyard and out the other side (note the 200-year-old fig tree that grows from the walls of the church). Turn right on the road and pass the primary school on the left.

You will pass a café on the right, where you can get lunch. Soon after there is a footpath to the left signed to Helford. Take this path and shortly cut through a gate to the left, then turn right along the right-hand edge of a field.

The footpath goes through a stile and on to a road. Turn left and immediately right on to another footpath which crosses a small field and then leads around the right-hand edge of the field to another stile at the far corner. Pass through this stile and into a woodland. This stretch of path can be muddy.

Helford village

This path leads down a small valley and along the right-hand side of a stream. A footpath leads off to the left; if you take it you will be on Walk 11 (page 98, at the point marked *). You could do this now; alternatively go to Helford for lunch, then come back to do Walk 11.

Continue down the right-hand side of the stream and straight on along the right-hand side of the creek once you reach the village of Helford. The road goes uphill and back to the car-park on the left. 2 hrs 45 mins

11 Helford to Frenchman's Creek

Beauty	****
Wildlife	***
Historical interest	***
General interest	*****
Distance	7 km (4½ miles)
Time	1 hour 30 mins
Walking conditions	Easy, can be muddy in places
Timing	Start at 11 a.m. to eat in pub or café on return to Helford (see Walk 10, page 95)
Start and end point	Helford pay-and-display car-park
Get to to start point	From Helston take A3083 on to the Lizard. Just after RNAS Culdrose turn left at roundabout, signed to St Keverne (B3293). Turn right at next roundabout; continue through Garras; after a further 1 mile turn left, signed to Manaccan. At T-junction in Newtown-in-St Martin turn right, then immediately left, signed to Manaccan. After a further 3 miles turn left, signed to Helford. Car-park on right before village
Toilets	Car-park at Helford

The ferry at Helford Point

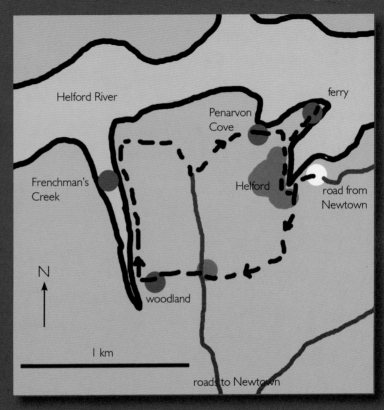

Helford River

ferry

Penarvon
Cove

Frenchman's
Creek

Helford

road from
Newtown

N

woodland

1 km

roads to Newtown

This is a short walk but one which takes in the rather atmospheric Frenchman's Creek made famous by Daphne Du Maurier. The walk passes Kestle Barton sculpture garden and café – a beautiful place to pause and enjoy a relaxing day. Its start and end point are at the lovely village of Helford, from where you can get a ferry boat to the other side of the river, or just relax and unwind. (This walk could be combined with Walk 10, pages 86–95, to make a longer circular route.)

Part of an art installation at Kestle Barton

path crosses the stream and leads up the other side of the small valley. Soon the path leads through a gate and along the right-hand side of a field. Through a larger gate you enter the hamlet of Kestle Barton, where there is a complex of self-catering accommodation and an exhibition space.

Kestle Barton is a contemporary arts venue. Have a look in the exhibition space and then wander through into the garden; there is no charge and the atmosphere is very informal. Here you can have tea and refreshments, and also walk on to their land which includes an orchard and new woodland. This facility is open from mid-April to October. (For details see www.kestlebarton.co.uk.)

From the car-park, walk out on to the minor road and turn right into Helford. Don't cross the footbridge by the ford on the right; instead continue along the left-hand side of the creek, and bear left on to the small road where there is a footpath sign to Manaccan. Go up a fairly steep hill and along the left-hand side of a thatched house. Continue along the footpath into the woods.

Soon there is a muddy stretch of path and bank on the right where it is possible to avoid some of the worst mud. Pause here to listen for nuthatches and jays in spring and autumn.

Turn right where there is a footpath sign (point marked * in Walk 10, page 95); this

Continue on the path and over a small road on to a little track that leads downhill into a woodland. The lower part of this woodland is packed with wild garlic (ramsons) in spring. Close to the creek the track bends left, and there is a footpath to the right signed to 'permissive path to Frenchman's Creek'; take this right turning. 45 mins

Wild garlic flowers in the spring at the head of Frenchman's Creek (above). The lovely twisted branch of a mature oak tree (right)

This path leads along the side of the creek. You will pass over a small bridge, and shortly after is a lovely old oak tree. Look at the common polypody (a type of fern) growing from its trunk and main branches. Turn right here where the path leads up some steps.

Frenchman's Creek is a great place to see. There are many oak trees dipping their

Old Quay, seen across Frenchman's Creek (above). A fallen oak in the creek (left)

leaves and branches into the salt water, which is quite unusual in most parts of the country. In fact, trees were growing here before the sea water came. The Helford, as well as the Carrick Roads and all of their tributaries, are part of a sunken valley, or ria. Unlike typical estuaries, these rias were formed by rivers creating a V-shaped river valley system. This

The path where the creek joins Helford River (above). Primroses and violets by the path (right)

was at a time when the sea levels were much lower than they are today. When we left the last Ice Age, sea levels began to rise and here the river valleys were flooded. Gradually the valleys silted up with mud from the rivers, and they now look a little like estuaries, but the steep-sided, wooded slopes leading down to the mud give the game away.

Ruined boat on Frenchman's Creek (left). The path passes under a sweet chestnut tree (right)

Soon there is a junction of footpaths. Turn right for a slightly quicker route*, or left for a more scenic one along the creek side, where you will pass under giant old holly trees growing beside a spring, and soon come down to a point where there is a ruined boat on a small beach. You can, with care, descend to this beach, but it is slippery and difficult to get back up! 1 hr

The path now leads uphill, passing a 'private gate' on the left. Soon you come to a small road; turn right here and go uphill. The small road emerges on the right-hand side of a field; continue up here; soon you will come to where the short cut emerges on to the same road*.

There is a bench on the left-hand side of this road, but don't attempt to turn left here. Continue along the road for another field, then turn left down a small road signed to Penarvon Cove. Continue down this road and at every junction of tracks take the downhill option. Soon you come to Penarvon Cove.

Cross the cove at the back of the beach and continue on the footpath up the hill on the opposite side. You will come to a T-junction with a small road; turn left here and continue to the bottom of the hill. Here at another T-junction I suggest a small detour to the left: you can walk along this short path to Helford Point where a ferry crosses to Helford Passage. To signal that you want to catch the ferry, you need to open out the circular sign above the quay: the ferryman will spot this and come over to pick you up.

This ferry has been operating since the Middle Ages when it would have been a vital link for communities. It is said that when farmers took their produce to markets in Fal-

Helford village at high tide (above). Looking up the creek in Helford from the footbridge (right)

mouth, the cart and the farmer travelled on the ferry while the horse swam along behind.

It is possible to cross and have lunch on the other side before returning if you wish. Otherwise return along the same path and through Helford village passing the Shipwright's Arms on the left.

This attractive public house is a great lunch venue with outdoor seating. It is a Grade II listed building with wheat-reed thatched roof and cob walls, probably dating to the eighteenth century.

Continuing further you will come back to the ford and footbridge. Cross the river here and turn left on the road which takes you back to the car-park. 1 hr 30 mins

12 Goonhilly Downs

Beauty	***
Wildlife	*****
Historical interest	*****
General interest	****
Distance	8 km (5 miles)
Time	2 hours 30 mins
Walking conditions	Usually easy, quite level, but can be very wet underfoot
Timing	Summer is best for flowers and insects (June to September)
Start and end point	Goonhilly Downs Natural England NNR car-park (free)
Get to to start point	From Helston take A3083 on to the Lizard. Just after RNAS Culdrose turn left at the roundabout, signed to St Keverne (B3293). Turn right at next roundabout, continue past Goonhilly Satellite Earth Station; after a further 400 m turn right into NNR car-park
Toilets	None

The viewing platform at RAF Dry Tree

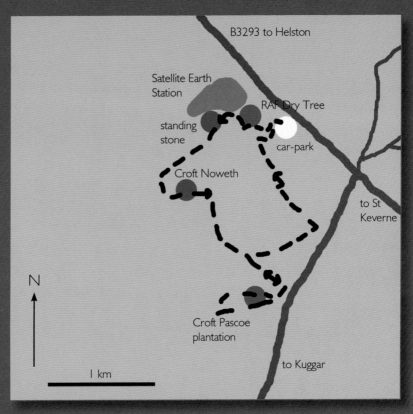

B3293 to Helston

Satellite Earth
Station

RAF Dry Tree

standing
stone

car-park

Croft Noweth

to St
Keverne

Croft Pascoe
plantation

to Kuggar

N

1 km

This is an area which can be wet; it can be windswept, and it can seem bleak; but choose the right day, take your time and have a good look around and you find a habitat that is rich in wildlife and is a very special site for flowers, including thousands of orchids in June. There aren't any facilities or cafés, so be prepared with packed lunch.

Arthur, the satellite dish, and heathers seen from the multi-user trail

Before you leave the car-park the most obvious landmark is the huge satellite dish, part of the Goonhilly Satellite Earth Station. This dish, named Arthur, was the first to be built here in 1962; its purpose was to track the Telstar satellite, and for the first time pictures from America were transmitted into British homes. Arthur set the standard, and soon other dishes, both here and around the world, were tracking and relaying signals.

There were over 60 dishes at Goonhilly, many named after characters in the Arthurian legends. Merlin was the largest, with a diameter of 32 m, and Arthur the heaviest, weighing 1,118 tonnes, yet with the capability to turn through 360° in less than three minutes.

A typical track across The Downs

In 2006, British Telecom announced that satellite work would move out of Cornwall, taking the dishes with it. Arthur will remain, however. It is now a Grade II listed structure standing proud over the surrounding heathland environment – a readily identifiable landmark, which is visible for miles around.

Goonhilly Downs form part of a NNR managed by Natural England. From the car-park there is a circular, all-weather trail suitable for wheelchairs.

From the car-park walk past the interpretation panel and turn left on the trail.

By walking only this trail we can get an impression of the types of flowers and wildlife

Left to right: Heath spotted orchid (most orchids on The Downs are these; they flower in June/July and vary in colour, many are almost pure white); fragrant orchid; Grayling butterfly, seen mid- to late summer

that can be seen across the Downs. As you walk around here and further afield, look out for flowers including Cornish heath, great burnet, heath spotted orchid, fragrant orchid, bog asphodel; butterflies including the grayling, and reptiles including common lizards.

Around this short trail are the remains of a Second World War RAF base – RAF Dry Tree. During the war, the Downs were of vital strategic importance. Radar operators from the Women's Auxiliary Air Force scanned the skies for enemy aircraft and, when spotted, fighter planes would be scrambled from nearby Predannack or Portreath.

Shortly turn right on to a main track; at the end turn left to climb the viewing platform, which gives great views over the downs.

The Downs is an area of heathland. This is not a natural habitat because it was formed when Neolithic people began to cut down forests and domesticate animals. These animals grazed where trees had been felled, and the result was what we see today. The management of the land is much the same as it was, with low levels of livestock grazing to keep on top of the scrubby vegetation.

Come back down from the platform and turn left, then left again immediately on to a small

Mounds that once held poles aloft to protect against German gliders landing in the Second World War (above). The Dry Tree Menhir (right)

path heading towards Arthur. Don't turn left through the kissing gate, but continue a further 25–30 m and then turn left on to a surfaced path alongside the perimeter fence of the Satellite Earth Station.

Soon you will see a significant standing stone, named the Dry Tree Menhir, and a Bronze Age barrow. Since the barrow is at the highest point on The Downs, it is now topped by a concrete triangulation point; make of that what you will!

Walk past the barrow and out on to The Downs through a kissing gate.

On the periphery of The Downs are six new wind turbines. Wind turbines have been here since 1993, but the fourteen old ones have been replaced by six much larger tur-

bines. The new ones stand some 107 m tall, and the new wind farm will generate three times as much power as the old one.

Don't take the bridleway but instead follow the path labelled as the Goonhilly Trail, which we will now follow for most of the way. This leads diagonally to the left of the bridleway. Shortly bear right again following the signs.

Scattered across Goonhilly are the remains of a Second World War defence. Because the area is relatively flat, it was thought that the Germans might attempt to land gliders here as part of an invasion force, so piles of earth were created into which were raised

Croft Noweth: Ruined farm building (left). The path cuts through land that was once farmed (right)

six-metre-tall poles. Though the poles have been taken away, the earth piles are still visible today. There are also further barrows, which are more substantial mounds of earth.

Look out for a left turning, again following the trail signs. Shortly the path cuts left through the 'wall' of Croft Noweth.

Situated within The Downs are a few crofts. Farming the land here was challenging with little reward, and some of these ruined farmsteads were once home to farmers who supplemented their livelihoods with a slightly less scrupulous form of activity. In 1821 the alleged highwayman John Barnicoat, of Croft Noweth, and John Thompson of Dry Tree Croft were hanged for robbing and murdering William Hancock who was on his way home from Helston market.

Go past the ruined farm building, through a beautiful tranquil wooded spot, and then out on to a main track. After a further 50 m turn right following the trail signs again. This heads towards Croft Pascoe Plantation. Keep the hedgerow on your right-hand side and you will soon see a kissing gate; go through this and on to the boardwalk.

To your right is a lovely shallow valley that hosts grasshopper warbler, Dartford warbler, nightjar and even hobby in summer. 1 hr

At the end of the boardwalk is an optional, recommended detour to explore Croft Pascoe Plantation. To do this take the right fork (if not take the left). Keep the fence to your right until you come to a barrow and a kissing gate into the plantation. You can go through here and wander freely, and return by the same gate.

Track through Croft Pascoe plantation (above), and dead trees around the plantation (right)

Shortly after the war the Forestry Commission began a trial to test the viability of converting the heathland into a giant fir tree plantation, consisting of many different types of tree. We should all be thankful that despite huge efforts to plough and fertilize the ground it was deemed unsuitable as a site to grow trees. The plantation remains at

The view of heather and the Satellite Earth Station from near Croft Pascoe

Croft Pascoe and is valuable wildlife habitat, but it will not be extended across the rest of Goonhilly. More recently a fire spread through the heath, killing many of the trees along the edge of this wood. It is a great place for birds, with nightjar and spotted flycatcher, for example. It is also excellent for insects, with many dragonflies hunting here on warm sunny days.

Retrace your steps to the board walk and then turn right. 2 hrs

Keep to the right of the hedge and cross the two board-walk bridges. The path turns left alongside the hedge and then meets a main track. Turn right, then almost immediately left, making for Arthur. When you reach a small sur-faced path turn right; keep right at every option to return shortly to the car-park. 2 hrs 30 mins